SAVE THE WORLD

In an Interesting Way

Meha Nicks
Saheli Basu

ISBN-13: 9781520723389

Cover design by: Meharima
Library of Congress Control Number: 2018675309
Printed in the United States of America

To my parents and all the readers

CONTENTS

INTRODUCTION

Look at the world in a different way. Feel the Breeze , it says ;Save The World in an interesting way.

FRONT COVER

SAVE THE WORLD

In an interesting way

"No matter how far we are,

No matter what situation we are in,

No matter how little we are able to offer,

All we can do together,is to Save the world"

SAHELI BASU

* * *

THE JOURNEY

(of Realization)

We,the people of this world ,
Let's take a look at the condition all around.

Doesn't it look destructed?
Don't you feel disheveled yourself?

I walk over to a window.
I urge you to come along with me!

Let's start by reflecting onto our surroundings.

Don't let the thoughts slip away!!

Let it arise and awaken your mind.

Let it come in contact with your soul.

Quitely!

Naturally!

Let it lead your way.

We always love to look at the beauty of the world.

At times ,we even like the mischievous and the notorious ways of it as well,

But never did we ever try to risk involving ourselves into the ground zero.

Doesn't it sound quite familiar ?

'Maybe or Maybe not'

It has now changed into a place that's far from the scenic views of land,valleys,mountains,rivers,oceans and waterfalls.

Instead it somehow buzzes with all sorts of noises.
Everything wrapped up in the confineness of the gadgets and only being captured by the eyes of the high-tech mobile device!

Our mortal eyes are a mere composition of nerves,muscles and fluid material,whose senses have been tackled to be subdued due
to the immense lack of utilization and interest .

Those times are long gone ,when we would walk in the grass...bare foot.
Doing nothing in particular but taking in the glory and cherishing the peace amongst the beauty of nature.

Never feeling alone or even if sometimes it ever seemed to happen and cause a bit of loneliness ,
we would have always found a friend beside us.

The greenary and the colorful floral bands in our front yard or the vase sitting on top of the table near the open window pane.
It called out to us.
Didn't it?

Let's go back.
Travelling through the nooks and corners of the memory lane.

We'll still find them ,in all their glory.
The once vast patch of the landscape ,is now scrapped and filled with the high-rise buildings.

Still if you are willing enough to search,you will find considerate amount of them when combined together,scanty however in a single spot or area.

In the shadows,
In the morning light,
It stands still.
The lone Banyan with it's braches hanging and supporting,
The palms,the figs and all otherss,watching their own reflection.

In the waterbodies,during the sunset...
The finned members bids their goodbye to the beams of life;
the cattle still waves at their avian friends ,in the hopes to meet again with the advent of daylight.

The mother earth still cradles ,rejuvinates and nourishes her children,irrespective of the condition they are in.

You can take a look at these with your own eyes.
All you'll need is YOU and that's your cue to find your very own WALK TO REMEMBER.
You only need to keep in none but YOU all along.

At the night the stars still twinkles,the moon still smiles and serenity ushers the life with open arms.

The nightangle still sings her lullaby to the babies.
The clouds still engages in a little game/play of hide and seek ,all throughtout the day and night.

It never lost hope.
It didn't ever lose.
It never gave up.

It's waiting for you to catch up.
Your friend!It never left your side.

'Look there!!'

A genuine,gentle ,charming range of creations .

They are a boon.
They are the bearers of life in itself.
The sustaiers of life across the globe,
The life savers.

Season still arrives but we have long given up on taking the subtle hints, too busy to notice the dew on the leaves , the latent spurt of the buds or the ripening of fruits , the slight alteration of the wind that blows,the whispers of the breeze and the fragrance of the monsoon showers .

Can you hear that!!
Hear what they are trying to say?
We used to liuve in our little houses surrounded by our family and friends.
Now we have moved away,upgraded to villas and apartments, from villages to cities.
We have changed our ways.
We have gone up from nothing to something.
We have immersed ourselves in shaping our careers,shaping our lives.
We have lost touch with our neighbours or the childhood friends.
We cut off ties for good and some for no reason at all.

We are all caught up in our own little worlds.
The world which seems colorful with the filters , the features of the digital age.
We choose how to paint our lives ,the scenery looks breathtaking but it's the photoshoped reality that looks like that.
No life is perfect !! Nor that it counts as imperfect !!
Nothing is perfect yet!!

The world is just too fast paced.
Our motivation is driven by the thoughts to not stand still ,just keep on running and running and keep up with it.

We must face the challenges and own the consequences of the same as well.

Time is knocking at the door.
We turn a blind eye to what's going on around ,what our deeds lead onto.

We tend to listen to music in full volume , turning the level so painfully high to escape .

Does it not sound relatable ?
Isn't it what you always do.

You are not the only one out there.
YOu are just one among them.

You ain't that special !
Not that special yet !!

I was there once.
I have been one of them in the past.

They kept saying "It's better late than never"

I realized that we are in suvh a misery that it probably needs volunteers to modify the saying in ways more than one.

"It's too late to think any longer.
Now is the time to act or you will regret forever"

That was my call.

I stepped down as one of them as a result.

I accepted my ignorant behaviour.

Looked back to my primary school days when we used to have ample provisions and resources for survival but didn't understand the value of them until after a decade .

Environment and it's treasures has got a new meaning
just the very moment I was enlightened , rather realized what went wrong or where it goes wrong.

I can understand the worth of every single thing now.

I am able to revive by the grace of the planet earth.
Every bit of it.

The trees, strong and stout serves us all , back and forth until the brink of it's death.
It's branches , barks ,roots, leaves ,flowers, fruits and all it's by products.
Even as the little sapplings or when it is getting decomposed.
It keeps on providing for all.

Countless instancess may have been rushing in front of your eyes , piercing your thoughts , pushing through the barriers of heart and mind.

"We can, just hear your inner voice," you will get the reply.

We can find ways, if we feel and understand the matter strongly.

SO LET'S JOIN HANDS AND

SAVE THE WORLD

In our very

own unique ways...

in an Interesting way......

Sanity is when we

Get to know ourselves...

Believe that you

are a gift to the world.

We are living in a state

Between

The act of awakening

And

The act of surrendering.

Spread

Love

&

Laughter .

Live,

Embrace positivity

and nourish life

in Style

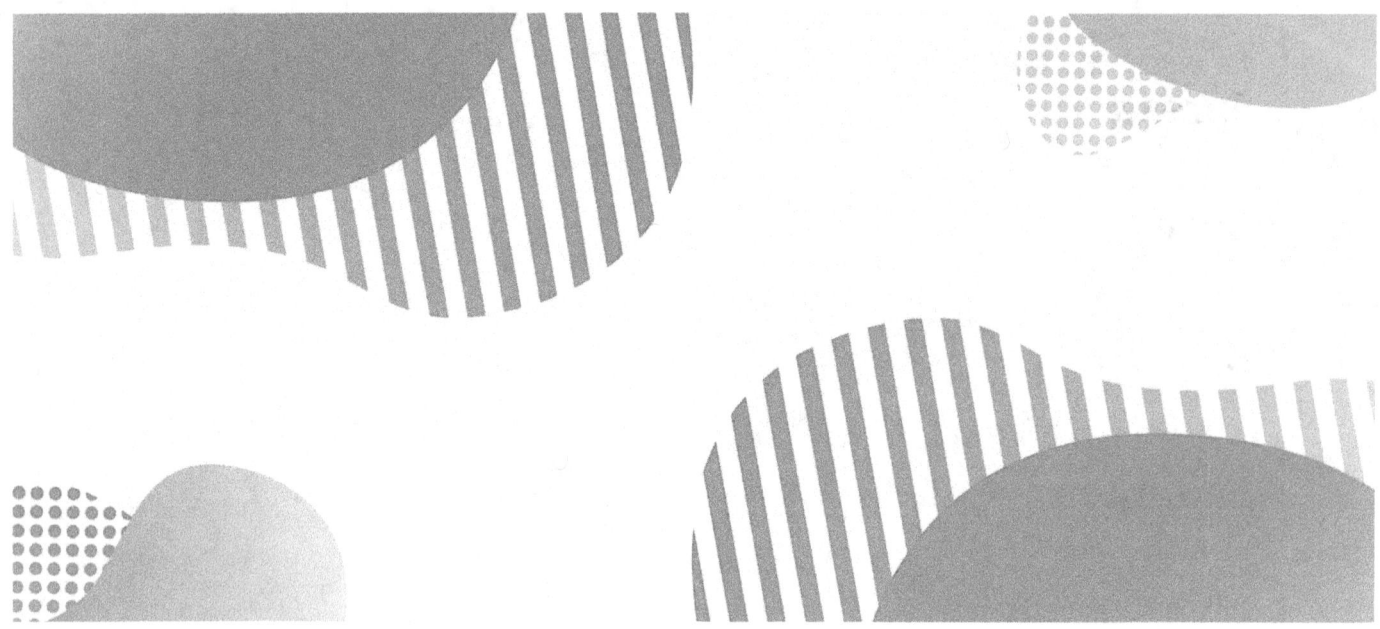

THE WORLD CALLED YOU

B e Yourself

Be you and

Never ever underestimate yourself.

Because the potential is hidden

and it is within YOU

✽ ✽ ✽

Dedicate to make the
atmosphere filled with
Joy & Hope

You possess everything

You are capable to perform the fieriest of things.

All of it ... ...

The Power ;

The Position;

The Questions;

The Answers ...

✻ ✻ ✻

All you want

All you need

Will be automatically

Uncover it's gateway

To welcome you

When You will

Be able to believe in

YOUR OWN SELF.

❋ ❋ ❋

YOU DON'T NEED ANY
RENOUNCIATION
YOU DON'T HAVE TO
WORRY ABOUT REJECTION

BECAUSE ALL OF US.....

RICH OR POOR

GOOD OR WORSE

ARE

GIVEN EQUAL CHANCES

TO

SEARCH OUR TRUTH

THE EYES WE HAVE

THE EARS WE HAVE

THE SENSES WE ARE

ALL AWARE OF......

IS NOTHING BUT AN

ILLUSION.

THE Great Lord....

Proves in dramatic ways

His truth to all.

He created men &

women alike

He created fire &

water side by side

He showed

The existence of

Contradictions

And their survival

Together ...

At the same time.

N ow,
Have you ever though!
Has it ever crossed your mind,

Why he created specially able-d people
along with so many people
Millions of them throughout the world....
In contrast to the billions
The So-called "Normal" People!

Okay

Okay

Okay

I will tell you ......

The courage

The passion

The confidence

The determination

Which always makes us awe in

RESPECT,

SURPRISE

&

ENDLESS PRAISE

Sometimes which the "So called Normal Bunch" lacks but never ever dare to confess their dearth of it.

We can conclude in general to the fact
that despite our structural and physical

differences we are all possessed with

Strengths and Weakness alike.

Whenever you mock someone's appearance
or their possessions
Remember you are on your own
disrespecting the creator , the maker of all....

So watch your steps accordingly

Never hurt anyone...
un reasonably...
un necessarily
whatsoever with or without knowing it's validity
Never betray an innocent, knowingly
Follow ideals, do not copy.

Respect individuality...
Respect yourself...
Respect everyone..
Keep in mind that no one is devoid of
hazards...
It requires a strong and steady mindset to
smile even in the hardest times.
SO DON'T FORGET TO SMILE

Everyone comes with baggage.

We have to search for someone who

Loves you enough to help you unpack.

T ruth of LIFE
The past is your lesson.
The present is your engine.
The future is your motivation.

Keep people in your life that truly
Love you,
Motivate you,
Encourage you,
Inspire you,
Enhance you,
And
Makes you happy.

IF YOU HAVE PEOPLE WHO DO NONE OF THE ABOVE,LET THEM GO.

A special something is indeed in store ...
WHEEL OF FORTUNE never stops it's mechanism .

That is why Change is the only constant in life.

If you like,you can always say:-
Dear God,
I woke up.
I am healthy.
I am alive.
Thank you.
I apologize for all my complaining.
I am truly grateful for all you have done.

Believe in your heart.
Believe with all your heart.
▯
A brief of EGO-SPIRIT Conversation:-
Ego says,
"Once everything falls into place,I'll feel peace."
Spirit says,
"Find your peace,and then everything will fall into place."

The fact is the truth,the reality and the inevitable,the invincible range of possibilities.

We can apply to serve our soul,
our source, and altogether The world,
our birthplace,our mother earth
and the divine abode!

* * *

ACKNOWLEDGEMENT

The feelings that summoned for recognization and expressed through the words herein.

ABOUT THE AUTHOR

Saheli Basu

An indigo child born on the
mid 90's in Kolkata,India.
She is the only child and "a
rebel with a wit".
The writers bug had been iching her for
about a decade which lead to the works published
as 'Meha Nick's' and is currently working on the
series "Enamored".

BOOKS BY THIS AUTHOR

Amazon Author Page

- Meeting With Eternity
- There is something between them
- Save The World
- Berty's Maggi
- Anthology Tide
- Enamored

BACK COVER

Save the world

IN AN INTERESTING WAY

Meha Nick's